Especially for

....

From

....

Date

....

© 2011 by Barbour Publishing, Inc.

Compiled and written by Shanna D. Gregor.

ISBN 978-1-61626-404-8

Published by Barbour Publishing, P.O. Box 719, Uhrichsville, OH 44683, www.barbourbooks.com

Our mission is to publish and distribute inspirational products offering exceptional value and biblical encouragement to the masses.

Member of the
Evangelical Christian
Publishers Association

Printed in China.

365

THINGS

You Should Know
About

LIFE

BARBOUR
PUBLISHING

Day 1

Life Is a Story

Your life is a story that only you can write, but everyone you meet can read it.

Day 2

The Essence of Life

Change is the essence of life.
Be willing to surrender what you
are for what you will become.

Day 3

Enjoying the Presence of God

Never forget to enjoy the presence of God. Life is always busy, so be careful that your quiet time doesn't become one of the many things on the list of things to do. Always remember, your first thing should be to spend some alone time with Him.

Day 4

Wings

No bird soars too high,
if he soars with his own wings.

WILLIAM BLAKE

Day 5

Shut Out the Voices

When you shut out the voices
of the day, you will discover how little
anything else but God matters. No one
knows the path He's chosen for you.
He points to the truth. He brings about
the results He destined for you
before the beginning of time.

Day 6

Rejoice Always

Rejoice in the Lord always.
I will say it again: Rejoice!

PHILIPPIANS 4:4 NIV

Day 7

The Basis of Life

Love should be the basis for every activity in the life of a believer. When you make a choice to accept Jesus, you choose to believe by faith. In the same way, we can choose love.

Day 8

Encouraging People

People who have an infectious laugh,
words of encouragement, and
an affectionate smile magnetically
pull others to them.

Day 9

Healthy Laughter

A sure way to stay healthy in every
area of your life is to deliberately
experience laughter. There's nothing
more refreshing and rewarding
than the moments spent laughing
so hard tears roll down your face.

Day 10

Every Joy

Every joy is gain
And gain is gain, however small.

ROBERT BROWNING

Day 11

A Good Marriage

Frequent laughter between a couple is
a good sign the marriage is working.

Day 12

The Word of Christ

*Let the word of Christ dwell in
you richly in all wisdom, teaching
and admonishing one another in psalms
and hymns and spiritual songs,
singing with grace in your
hearts to the Lord.*

COLOSSIANS 3:16 NKJV

Day 13

Imagination

Imagine—you were a thought, an idea
with grand purpose, before God ever
breathed life into the first man.

Day 14

The Importance of Laughter

Laughter can lighten your load.

Day 15
Don't Do It

Never lick a sharp knife.

Day 16

The Importance of Reading

I read my eyes out and can't read half enough. . . . The more one reads the more one sees we have to read.

JOHN ADAMS

Day 17

Encourage One Another

*But encourage one another day
after day, as long as it is still called
"Today," so that none of you will be
hardened by the deceitfulness of sin.*

HEBREWS 3:13 NASB

Day 18

Time Investment

If you died today, the company you work for could easily replace you. The family you love and leave behind will miss you for the rest of their lives. Consider where you invest your time, and make it a healthy balance focused on the things that matter most.

Day 19

Common Sense

Most of the time what you are
looking for is right in front of you.

Day 20

First-Rate Version

Always be a first-rate version
of yourself, instead of a second-rate
version of somebody else.

JUDY GARLAND

Day 21

The Puzzle of Life

In your personal puzzle of life,
don't force the pieces together.
If the pieces are meant to fit, they
will come together in their own
season as their design is revealed
to you—one piece at a time.

Day 22

Silence Is Dangerous

In some causes silence is dangerous;
so if any know of conspiracies
against their country or king,
or any that might greatly
prejudice their neighbor,
they ought to discover it.

SAINT AMBROSE

Day 23

My Heart's Delight

*When your words came, I ate them;
they were my joy and my heart's
delight, for I bear your name, LORD God
Almighty. I never sat in the company
of revelers. . . . I sat alone because
your hand was on me and you
had filled me with indignation.*

JEREMIAH 15:16–17 NIV

Day 24

The Frosting in Life

Friendship is the frosting between
the layers of life. It adds sweetness
and flavor between each
season of your life.

Day 25

The Right Thing

It's easier to say you have integrity
than to act on it. The ultimate test
rests in your decision to pursue
the right thing even if it costs
you more than you want to pay.

Day 26

Recognizing the Hurt

There are times when people
don't really want to fight,
but hope that the argument will
help you recognize their hurt.

Day 27

Faithful Words

God gave us words to frame our world with faith, just like He framed the world we live in with His own words. He commanded light to be—and light was. When we learn to be faithful with our words by speaking words we truly believe, we'll see our circumstances change.

Day 28

Praising God

When we refuse to throw in the towel,
the enemy has to accept failure.
Praising God in the midst of trials
demonstrates just exactly how
untouchable we are. The devil has
to give up. It's never easy to hold on,
but if you stay determined,
you win—he becomes the quitter.

Day 29

Forgiveness Is an Act

Forgiveness is an act of the will,
and the will can function regardless
of the temperature of the heart.

CORRIE TEN BOOM

Day 30

Tip for Tall People

If you happen to have short people
living in the house, don't put things
on top of the refrigerator.

Day 31

Tip for Short People

If you want to keep ice cream
all for yourself, put it on the bottom
shelf of the freezer. Taller people
don't look there. Ever.

Day 32

Think Twice

Think twice and speak once—if at all.

Day 33

A Miracle Word

*Every word you give me is a miracle
word—how could I help but obey?
Break open your words, let the light
shine out, let ordinary people see the
meaning. Mouth open and panting,
I wanted your commands
more than anything.*

PSALM 119:129–131 MSG

Day 34
Words of Love

Words of love and affirmation
can heal the deepest scars.

Day 35

Ancient and Latter Times

Ask counsel of both times—of the
ancient time what is best, and of
the latter time what is fittest.

Francis Bacon

Day 36

A Heart That Lives Long

A heart, light and filled
with laughter, lives long.

Day 37

Think Before You Act

Think before you act and then, when you do act, take full ownership of your actions—good or bad. Success is easy to own, but when your actions lead to failure, take responsibility.

Day 38

Birthday Presents

There are 364 days when you might get un-birthday presents, and only one for birthday presents, you know.

LEWIS CARROLL

Day 39

An Ounce of Foolishness

As dead flies cause even a bottle of perfume to stink, so a little foolishness spoils great wisdom and honor. A wise person chooses the right road; a fool takes the wrong one.

ECCLESIASTES 10:1 NLT

Day 40

Get Started

The best way to get
started is to take a step.

Day 41

Strong People

Happy are all free peoples, too strong to be dispossessed. But blessed are those among nations who dare to be strong for the rest!

ELIZABETH BARRETT BROWNING

Day 42
Face Reality

Life is not fair, no matter how much you want it to be. Adjust your expectation and it will be easier to face reality.

Day 43

Listen First and Speak Second

Having the discipline to listen first
and speak second will win you the
respect of others. They will come
to realize that when you speak,
you truly have something to say.

Day 44

Love Is a Choice

When you perceive love as an emotion,
it gives the mistaken impression that
you can only love if you feel loving.
When you realize love is a choice, it
empowers you to express love no matter
what happens, no matter how people
respond, no matter how you feel.

Day 45

Uphold My Steps

You have tested my heart;
You have visited me in the night;
You have tried me and found nothing;
I have purposed that my mouth shall not
transgress. Concerning the works
of men, by the word of Your lips,
I have kept away from the paths of the
destroyer. Uphold my steps in Your
paths, that my footsteps may not slip.

PSALM 17:3–5 NKJV

Day 46

The Big Picture

See the big pictures with a
wide-angle lens, but don't be critical.
Overlook the small errors, encourage
much, and correct very little.

Day 47

Affection

Affection is responsible for
nine-tenths of whatever solid
and durable happiness
there is in our lives.

C. S. LEWIS

Day 48

Take the Time to Grieve

It's perfectly normal to feel angry,
depressed, bitter, and lonely
when you lose a loved one.
Take your time and grieve.

Day 49

Cry Out to God

When you're tempted to hold a pity party in moments when your circumstances seem more than you can bear, cry out to God. It's okay if He feels far away. You can trust that He is there. You just can't hear Him because your own heart is shouting—drowning Him out.

Day 50

The Little Stuff

Don't get lost in the little stuff.
Turn friction into momentum.
It will help you focus on what
matters most and help you stay
determined to reach your goal.

Day 51

Of This World

If anyone loves the world, the love of the Father is not in him. For all that is in the world, the lust of the flesh and the lust of the eyes and the boastful pride of life, is not from the Father, but is from the world.

1 JOHN 2:15–16 NASB

Day 52

Never Quit

If you miss the first plane,
take the next one. Never quit—
never give up on your dream.

Day 53

My Soul

For it was not into my ear you whispered, but into my heart. It was not my lips you kissed, but my soul.

JUDY GARLAND

Day 54

Happiness Is a Choice

Happiness is a choice.
Discover the things that make
you happy and dedicate your life
to enjoying them every day.

Day 55

Words of Wisdom

He who trims himself to suit everyone
will soon whittle himself away.

RAYMOND HULL

Day 56

The Courage to Grow Up

It takes courage to grow up
and become who you really are.

E. E. CUMMINGS

Day 57

The Wise in Heart

The wise in heart are called discerning, and gracious words promote instruction. . . . The hearts of the wise make their mouths prudent, and their lips promote instruction. Gracious words are a honeycomb, sweet to the soul and healing to the bones.

PROVERBS 16:21, 23–24 NIV

Day 58

Learn

Learn to. . .be what you are,
and learn to resign with a good
grace all that you are not.

HENRI FREDERIC AMIEL

Day 59

Love and Hurt

I have found the paradox, that if you love until it hurts, there can be no more hurt, only more love.

MOTHER TERESA

Day 60

Check the Mirror

Look good coming and going.
Use a mirror to check your back
before leaving the house.

Day 61

Forgive and Forget

Are you willing to forgive but
not forget? The true measure of
forgiveness includes letting go.
The refusal to forget indicates
something not truly forgiven.
God's forgiveness forgets.

Day 62

God's Restoration

No matter what loss you have suffered,
God's restoration is never incomplete.
He covers all the bases. Somehow,
somewhere, He makes all things right.

Day 63

Family Dinners

Families around dinner tables are fast becoming a lost art. You can put some creativity back into mealtime with conversation and quality time around the table. If you can't do it daily, make it a weekly event, setting aside one meal a week for you and yours.

Day 64

On All Things True. . .

*Summing it all up, friends, I'd say
you'll do best by filling your minds
and meditating on things true, noble,
reputable, authentic, compelling,
gracious—the best, not the worst;
the beautiful, not the ugly; things
to praise, not things to curse.*

PHILIPPIANS 4:8 MSG

Day 65

God's Languages

Tears are a language God
understands; praise is a language
that puts Him in command.

Day 66

Fathers and Daughters

To a father growing old,
nothing is dearer than a daughter.

EURIPIDES

Day 67

Remain Grateful

You set yourself above
disappointment if you expect
nothing from people,
but remain grateful for everything!

Day 68

The Best Audience

God is the best audience you'll ever have; He's the best listener that exists. He is there anytime you want to talk or if you just want to sit and listen. You can glean lifetimes of wisdom when you set your affections on Him.

Day 69

Spend Time Listening

Spend time listening to the senior
citizens in your life. Ask them about
their childhood and what they
would do differently if they
could do it over again.

Day 70

Discover People's Hearts

Discover people and learn who they are. Never assume you know them until you've seen their heart.

Day 71

Darkness into Light

You, LORD, keep my lamp burning;
my God turns my darkness into light.

PSALM 18:28 NIV

Day 72

Impossibility

It's close to impossible to just spend a twenty-dollar bill at discount clubs.

Day 73

A Man's Reach

Ah, but a man's reach
should exceed his grasp,
Or what's a heaven for?

ROBERT BROWNING

Day 74

Be Available to Help

When it comes time to move and you need help moving, why is it that your family and friends always have other plans? Be available to help others, and they will return the favor.

Day 75

Teaching by Example

Sometimes you need to teach
others (through example) how
they should treat you.

Day 76

Past and Future

Your past experiences can influence
who you are, but you choose how that
influences you and who you become.

Day 77

Today

Today is a good day
to believe in miracles.

Day 78

A Time. . .

To everything there is a season, a time for every purpose under heaven. . . . A time to weep, and a time to laugh; a time to mourn, and a time to dance.

Ecclesiastes 3:1, 4 NKJV

Day 79

Every Day

Commit your waking
moments to God every day.

Day 80
Fate

I do not believe in a fate that
falls on men however they act;
but I do believe in a fate that
falls on them unless they act.

G. K. CHESTERTON

Day 81

God's Provision

King David was in awe of God.
He seemed overwhelmed by God's
purpose, plans, and provision for
his life. Have you ever stopped and
thought about where you've been
with God, and where you might
have ended up without Him?

Day 82

A Bedtime Snack

Buttermilk and corn bread
is a great bedtime snack—
especially when it's shared.

Day 83

Losing Perspective

You can lose perspective sometimes, but it only takes a jolt from the circumstances of life that takes your breath away, and then you realize some of the little things really just don't matter.

Day 84

God's Correction

But don't, dear friend, resent God's discipline; don't sulk under his loving correction. It's the child he loves that GOD corrects; a father's delight is behind all this.

PROVERBS 3:11–12 MSG

Day 85

Housing Jesus

If Jesus lives in your heart, make
sure you're treating your body as
the housing of a special guest.

Day 86

Open Doors

When one door of happiness closes,
another opens; but often we look
so long at the closed door that
we do not see the one which
has been opened for us.

HELEN KELLER

Day 87

Open Your Arms

Open your arms wide, squeeze tight, and love no matter what!

Day 88

An Encouraging Word

Never underestimate the power of
an encouraging word. Deliberately
choose to make someone's day.

Day 89

Sparkle!

There are those people who sparkle.
When you see them, they shine with
expectation of the goodness that is
going to happen at any moment. Choose
to be one of those people each day.
Fill the life of others with your light!

Day 90

Listen to the Answer

"You had no sooner started your prayer when the answer was given. And now I'm here to deliver the answer to you. You are much loved! So listen carefully to the answer, the plain meaning of what is revealed."

DANIEL 9:23 MSG

Day 91

A Priceless Treasure

God has trusted you with a
priceless treasure—your children.
He depends on you to give them
the best of yourself and provide
them with an understanding
of His goodness and love.

Day 92

Bringing Up a Child

There is just one way to bring up a child in the way he should go and that is to travel that way yourself.

ABRAHAM LINCOLN

Day 93

Let Your Light Shine

No matter the circumstances, let your light shine. Your life is a living letter of God's favor and goodness. Choose to tell His story through your words and actions on every road you travel.

Day 94

Being a Christian

Being a Christian is not about following
the rules, but about following God.
Jesus said, "YOU SHALL LOVE THE LORD
YOUR GOD WITH ALL YOUR HEART, AND WITH
ALL YOUR SOUL, AND WITH ALL YOUR MIND"
(Matthew 22:37 NASB).

Day 95

Faith and Fear

Faith magnifies the Lord in the face
of adversity. Fear wants you to focus
on the possibility that somehow you
missed it—but faith stands strong
and sees the salvation of the Lord.

Day 96

Think Again

When you think you
can't, think again.

Day 97

Love

Of all the things you can do in life,
the one thing that matters
most is that you loved.

Day 98

A Just Cause

When a just cause reaches its flood-tide, as ours has done in that country, whatever stands in the way must fall before its overwhelming power.

CARRIE CHAPMAN CATT

Day 99

The Lessons in Life

Life is an up-and-down experience.
We'd all love to live on the
mountaintops, but it's the low
points—the valleys—where you grow
and discover the big lessons in life.

Day 100

Dance in the Rain

Never decide that you're too old
or too stiff to dance in the rain.

Day 101
The Simple Things

The simple little things like playing
a game of checkers, holding
someone's hand, or listening
to their favorite story can be the
biggest investment you will ever make.

Day 102

The Harder the Fall

*First pride, then the crash—the
bigger the ego, the harder the fall.*

PROVERBS 16:18 MSG

Day 103

The Best Gift

Letting go of your children can
be the hardest thing you've ever
done, but the best gift you
can possibly give them.

Day 104

Avoid Procrastination

To make the most of your time,
do the things you like least, first.

Day 105

The Antidote to Frustration

The antidote to frustration is a calm
faith, not in your own cleverness, or in
hard toil, but in God's guidance.

NORMAN VINCENT PEALE

Day 106

Time as Currency

Think of time as a currency.
Where do you spend it? Who or what
will you give your time to today?

Day 107

A Healthy Life

The power of living a healthy life is determined by the positive and negative habits you establish. To achieve your goals, eliminate habits that would take away from your success, and surround yourself with the support that encourages you to add to your life.

Day 108

A Level Head

A level head prevails when
you are proactive, not reactive.

Day 109

100 Years from Now

Before acting on impulse when you're upset , as yourself a simple question: Will this matter 100 years from now?

Day 110

It's Okay to Fail

It's okay to fail a number of times
until you eventually succeed.

Day 111

A Prudent Question

A prudent question is
one half of wisdom.

FRANCIS BACON SR.

Day 112

All Your Heart

Wherever you go,
go with all your heart.

CONFUCIUS

Day 113

Talent

Everyone has a talent.
Sometimes it just takes longer for them
to find it and share it with others.

Day 114

Saying No

Saying no sometimes doesn't
make you nasty, cruel, or unkind;
it just makes you wise.

Day 115

Take Note of This:

My dear brothers and sisters, take note of this: Everyone should be quick to listen, slow to speak and slow to become angry, because human anger does not produce the righteousness that God desires.

JAMES 1:19–20 NIV

Day 116

As You Are

Let the world know you as you are,
not as you think you should be,
because sooner or later, if you are
posing, you will forget the pose,
and then where are you?

FANNY BRICE

Day 117

The Truth Is Incontrovertible

The truth is incontrovertible—
malice may attack it, ignorance may
deride it, but in the end, there it is.

WINSTON CHURCHILL

Day 118

What You Want

If what you want requires deceit, manipulation, or harsh words to attain, it's not worth having.

Day 119

Loved Unconditionally

Every day remind yourself
that you deserve
to be loved unconditionally.

Day 120

Practice Hospitality

Make your home a
safe place to land.

Day 121

The Word of Truth

Warn them before God against quarreling about words; it is of no value, and only ruins those who listen. Do your best to present yourself to God as one approved, a worker who does not need to be ashamed and who correctly handles the word of truth.

2 TIMOTHY 2:14–15 NIV

Day 122

Courage Is Contagious

It is not the absence of fear,
but the willingness to face your
fear and embrace your faith.

Day 123

Sit Down

It takes a lot of nerve to start
something new that wasn't there
before, to sit down at the empty
table and wait to see who
sits down with you.

Day 124

Dreams Are Fragile Things

Say nevermore
That dreams are fragile things.
What else endures
Of all this broken world
save only dreams!

DANA BURNET

Day 125

A High Level

The world is full of people who
barely get by. Don't settle for the
minimum requirements. Seek a high
level of excellence by doing more than is
expected and your results will produce
promotion, reward, and success
in everything you do.

Day 126

Keep Moving Forward

The way we navigate the difficulties
in life is not to tie a knot in our rope
and hang on, but instead don't stop.
Keep moving forward and allow
the grace of God to fuel us to get
through what we're going through.

Day 127

If You Become a Parent

If you become a parent, remember:
the most priceless ornaments that
can ever adorn your neck are
the arms of your children.

Day 128

Another Step

Courage is the willingness
to step into the unfamiliar,
and then take another step.

Day 129

Giving Away Your Heart

Once you give your heart to another it no longer belongs to you. So be sure it goes to someone you can trust to keep it for you.

Day 130

The Triumph of Evil

The only thing necessary
for the triumph of evil is for
good men to do nothing.

EDMUND BURKE

Day 131

A Road without Challenges

A road without challenges or obstacles may be very easy to navigate but seldom takes you anywhere worthwhile in life.

Day 132

A Wise Woman

A man becomes everything his
wife expects. She holds his future
in her heart. A wise woman uses her
power to influence his dreams to
reality with words of affirmation.

Day 133

The Unbreakable Bonds of Sisterhood

If you have ever observed or experienced the unbreakable bonds of sisterhood, then you have most likely found that it does not matter how the bond of sisterhood is formed—by blood or by fire, friendship or fate—once the two hearts are joined, it becomes an everlasting covenant.

Day 134

Guarding You

*For He will give His angels
charge concerning you,
to guard you in all your ways.*

PSALM 91:11 NASB

Day 135

Faith and Hope

Hope is an earnest expectation
of what can be. Faith is believing
God will get you there.

Day 136

A Sign

A man's life is interesting
primarily when he has failed—
I well know. For it's a sign
that he tried to surpass himself.

GEORGES CLEMENCEAU

Day 137

Body and Soul

Your body and soul require
refueling to keep you ready to live
your life on purpose each day.

Day 138

In Their Father's Arms

It's quite an awesome thing to see the healing that takes place when children are held tightly in their father's arms.

Day 139

All Dogs Know

All dogs know if you stare
at someone long enough, you'll
eventually get what you want.

Day 140

God's Promise

"Abraham is going to become
a large and strong nation. . . . Yes,
I've settled on him as the one to train
his children and future family to
observe GOD's way of life, live kindly
and generously and fairly, so that
GOD can complete in Abraham
what he promised him."

GENESIS 18:18–19 MSG

Day 141

The Child in All of Us

A peanut butter and jelly sandwich with a cold glass of milk can bring out the child in all of us.

Day 142

Unanswered Prayer

Our Lord never referred to
unanswered prayer; He taught
that prayers are always answered.
He ever implied that prayers were
answered rightly because of the
heavenly Father's wisdom.

OSWALD CHAMBERS

Day 143

God's Grace

One day you'll find out,
with the experience of years,
that you were either smarter
than you thought, or that
God's grace reached much
deeper into man's stupidity
than you ever dreamed!

Day 144

The Best Memories

The best memories of life's
classroom are the education
received while facing the
most difficult of times.

Day 145

The Simple Things

Celebrate the simple things with laughter: ice cream on the tip of your nose, car keys dropped into a pile of snow, and the realization that you are wearing mismatched shoes to your sister's wedding.

Day 146

An Honest Witness

An honest witness tells the truth, but a false witness tells lies. The words of the reckless pierce like swords, but the tongue of the wise brings healing. Truthful lips endure forever, but a lying tongue lasts only a moment.

PROVERBS 12:17–19 NIV

Day 147

Space for Love

A heart filled by God
has infinite space for love.

Day 148

Talking to God

Talking to men for God
is a great thing, but talking to
God for men is greater still.

E. M. Bounds

Day 149

An Extra Set of Hands

Sometimes the greatest blessings
come when you're willing to ask for
help, especially when you realize that
others are more than willing to
offer an extra set of hands.

Day 150
True Joy

You can do things your way or by
God's perfect design. True joy comes
when you choose to live your life
through God's perspective.

Day 151

The Greatest Life Lessons

Those with the greatest life
lessons are people who are committed
to never stop learning and are always
willing to be taught no matter how
old or young the teacher.

Day 152

The Simple Truth

*"Because you're not yet taking
God seriously," said Jesus. "The simple
truth is that if you had a mere kernel
of faith, a poppy seed, say, you would
tell this mountain, 'Move!' and it
would move. There is nothing you
wouldn't be able to tackle."*

MATTHEW 17:20 MSG

Day 153

Rest in God

There is little to worry about.
The truth—there is freedom from
everything when you rest in God.
The more you lean into His higher
purpose, the less you try to
work it out on your own.

Day 154

Freedom

To be what no one ever was,
To be what everyone has been:
Freedom is the mean of those
Extremes that fence all effort in.

MARK VAN DOREN

Day 155

Find Peace in God's Word

God's Word can bring balance after a difficult day. Allow the Bible to cleanse your emotions, clear your mind, redirect your will, and stimulate your spirit. When the world steps on your last nerve, take some time and get alone with the Bible and find peace.

Day 156

Loving Others

It's hard to love others when they disappointment you. When you find relationships are most difficult, remember how far God reached out to extend His love to you. Then ask Him to help you follow His example by reaching out to them.

Day 157

An Excellent Friend

Listening is perhaps the most
important part of relationships.
An excellent friend doesn't just look
at the other person, waiting for
them to stop talking so they can
start talking. They truly want to
hear what you have to say.

Day 158

Human Approval

*When push came to shove they
cared more for human approval
than for God's glory.*

JOHN 12:43 MSG

Day 159

Willing to Fail

The greatest minds in the world were
willing to fail until they succeeded.

Day 160

The Brave Man

The brave man is not he who feels
no fear, For that were stupid and
irrational; But he, whose noble soul
its fears subdues, And bravely dares
the danger nature shrinks from.

JOANNA BAILLIE

Day 161

Evil Company

Do not be deceived:
"Evil company corrupts good habits."

1 CORINTHIANS 15:33 NKJV

Day 162

Perceptions Are Individual

Perceptions are individual.
Three people can look at the same
object and see three different things.
Assume there is always a different
way to look at something and
entertain other viewpoints.

Day 163

Triumphs and Disappointments

Don't let your triumphs go
to your head or your
disappointments go to your heart.

Day 164

Trust in the Lord

Some trust in chariots and some in horses, but we trust in the name of the Lord our God.

PSALM 20:7 NIV

Day 165
A Kiss Will Heal

A kiss will heal the little hurts.
A wounded heart requires love,
tenderness, understanding,
compassion, and time to heal.

Day 166

The Approval of God

Others may not approve of you,
or of what you are doing. But keep your
focus and press on. We desire the
approval of God—not men.

Day 167

Character

Of all the properties which belong
to honorable men, not one is so highly
prized as that of character.

HENRY CLAY

Day 168

Home

Home should be the one place
where you feel safe and protected
from the hard things of life—where
you share memories, stories,
and laughter with your family.

Day 169

Dirty Dishes

Thank God for dirty dishes,
They have a tale to tell.
While others are going hungry,
We're eating very well.
With home and health and happiness,
I shouldn't want to fuss.
For by this stack of evidence,
God's very good to us.

UNKNOWN

Day 170
Success Stories

The greatest success stories are
told about someone who chooses
to believe they could when
everyone said it was impossible.

Day 171

Stand Your Ground

*With all this going for us, my dear,
dear friends, stand your ground.
And don't hold back. Throw yourselves
into the work of the Master,
confident that nothing you do for
him is a waste of time or effort.*

1 Corinthians 15:58 msg

Day 172

Role Model

Although you may not realize it, people are watching you. Whether you like it or not, you are a role model to someone.

Day 173

The Architect of Decay

He who rejects change is the architect of decay. The only human institution which rejects progress is the cemetery.

HAROLD WILSON

Day 174

If You Don't. . .

If you don't go after what you want,
you'll never have it. If you don't ask,
the answer is always no. If you
don't step forward, you're
always in the same place.

Day 175
Comfort and Safety

What comfort we find in feeling safe with someone. We can speak without quantifying our words, sharing them without restraint. We are free knowing they will keep what is worth savoring and the rest will be blown away with the wind, completely forgotten.

Day 176

Money

Choose to make money serve you,
instead of spending your
life serving money.

Day 177

Neighbors

*"Let each one of you speak truth
with his neighbor," for we are
members of one another.*

Ephesians 4:25 NKJV

Day 178
True Wealth

A man's true wealth is
what he leaves behind.

Day 179

Some Men

There are some men who lift the age they inhabit, till all men walk on higher ground in that lifetime.

MAXWELL ANDERSON

Day 180

What Your Heart Looks Like

The things you talk most about
are the things closest to your heart.
Listen to your words and you'll
find a true picture of what your
heart truly looks like.

Day 181

No Matter What

No matter what is behind you,
God is forgiving. No matter what
is before you, God is able!

Day 182

Heart's Passion

Passion can be described as
wanting something so badly that you're
willing to sacrifice anything to have it.
What is the fuel that fires the
passion in your heart?

Day 183

Prayer

*"When two of you get together
on anything at all on earth and make
a prayer of it, my Father in
heaven goes into action."*

MATTHEW 18:19 MSG

Day 184
God's Plan

You can gain advice from the world's wisest men about what direction to take your life, but it is all for nothing if you go in the wrong direction. Consider God's plan and follow His direction, and you can have assurance that your path is the right one.

Day 185

Greatness

There was never a nation great until
it came to the knowledge that it had
nowhere in the world to go for help.

CHARLES DUDLEY WARNER

Day 186

Identification

All dogs know to not go
out without identification.

Day 187

Words

If words were currency,
how are you spending them?

Day 188

Thought

If you think about one thought long enough, you give it voice. Once it has a voice, it leads to actions. Once you act, it becomes your daily behavior which then leads to a permanent part of your character. And finally, that thought has become your destiny.

Day 189
The Way

*Whether you turn to the right
or to the left, your ears will hear
a voice behind you, saying,
"This is the way; walk in it."*

ISAIAH 30:21 NIV

Day 190

Communication

Communication with God exists in
those powerful moments when you
honestly and openly express to Him
who you are—and who He is to you.

Day 191

An Unknown Future

Never be afraid to trust an
unknown future to a known God.

CORRIE TEN BOOM

Day 192
A Home

Things that make a house a home:

an embracing welcome
a final good-bye
tears
laughter
knowing there is safety and
comfort within those four walls.

Day 193

An Appreciation

Take an appreciation tour of your life.
What are you thankful for? Make a
list focusing on what you have
instead of what is missing.
Celebrate the little things today.

Day 194

Parenting

Parenting a child is one of life's
greatest tools for learning. It will
also stretch you beyond the limits and
can cause you to grow beyond
your wildest dreams.

Day 195

Listening

*Then the LORD came
and stood and called as at
other times, "Samuel! Samuel!"
And Samuel said, "Speak,
for Your servant is listening."*

1 SAMUEL 3:10 NASB

Day 196

Backing Up Files

Backing up your important files in your computer is vital to maintaining the things you want to keep. The same can be said about your relationships. Take time to invest time and energy in the ones you love by making memories that will last for all eternity.

Day 197

Answers

In every petition, be filled with the
assurance that prayer, offered in loving
faith in the living God, will bring
certain and abundant answer.

ANDREW MURRAY

Day 198

Daily Patience

Show the same patience for others
that God shows you on a daily basis.

Day 199

The Passing of Time

With the passing of time, it becomes
more evident that we cannot clearly
see where we are if we're unwilling
to reflect on where we've been.

Day 200

Faith

When faith speaks, fear has no choice but to turn tail and run.

Day 201

Wavering

A person with divided loyalty is as unsettled as a wave of the sea that is blown and tossed by the wind. Such people should not expect to receive anything from the Lord. Their loyalty is divided between God and the world, and they are unstable in everything they do.

JAMES 1:6–8 NLT

Day 202
Band-Aids

Band-Aids are made for boo-boos—
real ones and even the ones you
can't see. Be willing to put them
on anything and everything
your kids want covered.

.

Day 203

Guilty

He declares himself guilty who
justifies himself before accusation.

PROVERB

Day 204

Give Thanks

Take time to give thanks.

Day 205

Go to God

When the going gets tough,
you can always go to God.

Day 206

Our Inner Fire

In everyone's life, at some time,
our inner fire goes out. It is then
burst into flame by an encounter with
another human being. We should
all be thankful for those people
who rekindle the inner spirit.

ALBERT SCHWEITZER

Day 207

In the Darkness

The light shines in the darkness,
and the darkness has not overcome it.

JOHN 1:5 NIV

Day 208

Inspiration

Look to others for inspiration
instead of validation.

Day 209

Developed Wings

God stirs up our comfortable nests,
and pushes us over the edge of them,
and we are forced to use our wings
to save ourselves from fatal falling. Read
your trials in this light, and see if your
wings are being developed.

HANNAH WHITALL SMITH

Day 210

Reach Your Goal

Don't get so concerned about
how far you have to go in order
to reach your goal that you forget
to applaud yourself for how far
you've already come.

Day 211

Smile!

It may be cliche, but it's absolutely true:
The quickest way to improve your
looks and your outlook is to smile.

Day 212

Be Who You Are

Be who you are and say what you feel,
because those who mind don't matter
and those who matter don't mind.

DR. SEUSS

Day 213

As I Pray

*As soon as I pray,
you answer me;
you encourage me by
giving me strength.*

PSALM 138:3 NLT

Day 214

A Little Appreciation

A little appreciation can
fuel someone's day.

Day 215

The Neglected Heart

The neglected heart will soon be
a heart overrun with worldly thoughts;
the neglected life will soon become
a moral chaos; the church that is
not jealously protected by mighty
intercession and sacrificial labors will
before long become the abode of
every evil bird and the hiding place
for unsuspected corruption.

A. W. Tozer

Day 216

Ask

Don't be afraid to
ask why—repeatedly.

Day 217

Less Stress

Life will prove much less
stressful when you really don't care
what other people think of you.

Day 218
Challenges

Refuse to allow others to limit
you with words of what you can't do;
instead, accept their negative words as
challenges and defy their limitations.

Day 219

Children of the Light

*For you are all children of the
light and of the day; we don't
belong to darkness and night.*

1 THESSALONIANS 5:5 NLT

Day 220

Be Careful

Be careful not to get so
busy working for God that
you miss His direction in
what He wants you to do.

Day 221

Hope and Confidence

Optimism is the faith that leads
to achievement. Nothing can be done
without hope and confidence.

HELEN KELLER

Day 222

Let Your Light Shine

Sometimes others need for
your light to shine in their lives
before they can truly see.

Day 223

Get On with Life

You can't change what is already done. Don't waste your time wishing things were different. Simply get on with life.

Day 224

A Wise Student

Most people want to talk about themselves. It is a wise student who asks questions of his mentor and is willing to listen and immediately apply what he hears.

Day 225

Be Willing to Listen

Sometimes the truth is hard to hear, but when it comes from a friend who truly loves you, be willing to listen and adjust so that you can reach your full potential.

Day 226

Strength from God

*God said this once and for all;
how many times have I heard it
repeated? "Strength comes
straight from God."*

PSALM 62:11 MSG

Day 227

Pursue Your Dream

Don't wait to pursue your dream.
Take a step today—however small—
toward it. Give it everything you've
got. What a waste to die with
the music still in you.

Day 228

Beyond Expectation

Faith expects from God what
is beyond all expectation.

ANDREW MURRAY

Day 229

Donate

Donate gently worn clothing
and toys to charities to help out
folks who have need.

Day 230

The Hearts of
Your Children

The greatest prizes you
could ever win are the
hearts of your children.

Day 231

Choose to Be Reconciled

Relationships die over the stupidest things. Proving who's right or wrong isn't worth the conflict and division. Stop keeping score—instead choose to be reconciled.

Day 232

Don't Fit In

Don't become so well-adjusted to your culture that you fit into it without even thinking. Instead, fix your attention on God. You'll be changed from the inside out.

ROMANS 12:2 MSG

Day 233

Be Unique!

Many work hard to be like everyone
else. The truth is, people are drawn
to those who are unique. Don't be
afraid to be a little different!

Day 234

A Famine of Life

There is a famine in America.
Not a famine of food,
but of love, of truth, of life.

MOTHER TERESA

Day 235

His Loving Arms

Listen to your heavenly Father's
voice and He will always lead you
back to His loving arms.

Day 236
Self Talk

It's okay to talk to yourself.
Tell yourself how special you are.
You have value that exceeds where you
are today. Let the potential God placed
within you take you to the destiny
He created you to achieve.

Day 237

Today

Brag about yourself today.

Day 238

Six Things God Hates

*Here are six things God hates,
and one more that he loathes with
a passion: eyes that are arrogant,
a tongue that lies, hands that murder
the innocent, a heart that hatches evil
plots, feet that race down a wicked
track, a mouth that lies under oath,
a troublemaker in the family.*

PROVERBS 6:16–19 MSG

Day 239

Don't Argue

Don't argue a speeding ticket if
you know you were in the wrong.

Day 240

A Responsible Adult

Living life as a responsible adult
means cleaning up your own mess.

Day 241

A Good Education

To give children a good education in manners, arts, and science is important; to give them a religious education is indispensable; and an immense responsibility rests on parents and guardians who neglect these duties.

NOAH WEBSTER

Day 242

Say You're Sorry

It's important to say you're sorry when you hurt someone. No matter how trivial it seems to you, it means a lot to the person and the relationship.

Day 243
The World

Don't go around saying the world owes you a living. The world owes you nothing. It was here first.

MARK TWAIN

Day 244

Death and Loss

The death of someone you love
changes you. You can allow that loss
to devastate and destroy; or you can
take your time, lean on God, and allow
Him to reconstruct the damage to your
heart. God restores us, if we will
let Him, when we are ready.

Day 245

Pray and Confess

*And I prayed to the LORD my God,
and made confession, and said,
"O Lord, great and awesome God,
who keeps His covenant and mercy
with those who love Him, and with
those who keep His commandments."*

DANIEL 9:4 NKJV

Day 246

Vitamin D

Vitamin D is important to your health.
Spend a few minutes each day in the sun
reading a book or just relaxing.

Day 247

Wait on God

In the rush and noise of life,
as you have intervals, step home
within yourselves and be still. Wait
upon God, and feel His good presence;
this will carry you evenly through
your day's business.

WILLIAM PENN

Day 248

A Hard Lesson

It may be a hard lesson,
but not everyone will like you.
Enjoy life with the ones who do.

Day 249

An Invisible God

We serve an invisible God who is always at work behind the scenes of our lives. When we take the time to stop and look, we can see Him at work within the simple places in our lives.

Day 250

Remember

Have you ever stopped and thought about where you've been with God and where you might have ended up without Him? Remember where you came from.

Day 251

All of My Sins

*In your love you kept me from
the pit of destruction; you have put
all my sins behind your back.*

ISAIAH 38:17 NIV

Day 252

God Forgives and Forgets

While we should learn
from our mistakes, God doesn't
want us to torture ourselves.
He is not a punisher. Through
forgiveness, God forgets.

Day 253

Marriage

Marriage was ordained
for a remedy and to increase the
world and for the man to help the
woman and the woman the man,
with all love and kindness.

WILLIAM TYNDALE

Day 254

Amazing Opportunities

Hold your head high and you'll
never miss the amazing opportunities
that come your way.

Day 255

Find a Solution

Anyone can create a problem,
but the one who finds a solution is
the one who finds success.

Day 256

Count the Cost

Count the cost before burning
a bridge in any relationship.
The bridge may become worn
and tattered, but sometimes it's
nice to go back and visit when
you find yourself close
to friendship again.

Day 257

Be Blessed

"For they are people blessed by the Lord, and their children, too, will be blessed. I will answer them before they even call to me. While they are still talking about their needs, I will go ahead and answer their prayers!"

Isaiah 65:23–24 NLT

Day 258

The Right Direction

God knows when you're not going the right direction, and He's never too busy to guide you back on course.

Day 259

The Flame of God

Give me the love that leads the way,
the faith that nothing can dismay,
the hope no disappointments tire,
the passion that will burn like fire;
Let me not sink to be a clod:
Make me Thy fuel, Flame of God.

AMY CARMICHAEL

Day 260

Find Encouragement

Constant negative news can drain you.
Find some encouragement each day to
energize you. Inspiration from Bible
reading is a great place to start.

Day 261

Make Music

Make music, or at least
experience it. Music is a language
the soul understands.

Day 262

A Decision

Love is not an emotion,
but a decision.

Day 263

Your Holy Hill

O LORD, who may abide in Your tent?
Who may dwell on Your holy hill?
He who walks with integrity,
and works righteousness,
And speaks truth in his heart.

PSALM 15:1–2 NASB

Day 264

Open Your Heart

It doesn't really matter what the
topic of discussion is when you're
spending time with those you love.
Opening your heart to them
is what matters most.

Day 265

Temptation

Temptations are a file which
rub off much of the rust of
our self-confidence.

FRANÇOIS FÉNELON

Day 266

Love Languages

People receive love in different ways.
The best gift you can give to those
you love is to express your love
in the way they'll understand.

Day 267

Be a Gentleman

It is still fashionable to be a
gentleman or a lady. Opening the car
door for a lady speaks volumes to her
worth and his personal integrity.

Day 268

A Choice to Make

Growing up doesn't happen just
because you get older, but it's a
choice you have to make.
Don't wait too long.

Day 269

Whatever You Ask

*"And whatever you ask in My name,
that I will do, that the Father may
be glorified in the Son. If you ask
anything in My name, I will do it."*

JOHN 14:13–14 NKJV

Day 270

The Creative Spirit

The creative spirit that God
put inside of you is always at work.
Let His creativity bring out
the best in you today.

Day 271

Faith and Obedience

Faith and obedience are bound
up in the same bundle. He that obeys
God trusts God; and he that trusts God
obeys God. He that is without faith
is without works; and he that is
without works is without faith.

CHARLES SPURGEON

Day 272

Good Sportsmanship

When you win or lose,
demonstrate good sportsmanship.

Day 273

Best Friends

The best friends you will ever have are the relationships you never expected—the ones that God brings.

Day 274

Working with His Strength

Your mind continually processes thoughts, new ideas, solutions, and creative ways of doing old things. That creative spirit God put inside you is always at work and can become overwhelming. Invite God to set the priorities for your day. Working within His strength lightens your load.

Day 275

Refuge

*Keep me safe, O God, for I
have come to you for refuge.*

PSALM 16:1 NLT

Day 276

A New Day

In the midst of a night season—
those times when life seems dark
and you feel alone, allow the hope
of God's goodness to restore His
light in your heart. A new day is
dawning and with it new strength
for the journey forward.

Day 277

Work and Pray

Pray, then, and work.
Work and pray.
And still again pray, and then work.
And so on, all the days of your life.
The result will surely be abundant
blessing. Whether you see much
fruit or little fruit, such kind of
service will be blessed.

GEORGE MÜLLER

Day 278

Wise Words

Don't just put wise words on
your wall for others to see,
but take them to heart and apply
them each day to your life.

Day 279

Material Possessions

No material possessions are
worth destroying a relationship
with family or friends.

Day 280

You Decide

Don't let others tell you what
is best for you. It's your life
and only you can decide.

Day 281

Babies and Animals

BEST FRIENDS, BUSINESS PARTNERS,
AND MATES ARE PEOPE WHO ARE KIND
TO BABIES AND ANIMALS.

Day 282

Invite Him In

Prayer opens the door to a relationship with God, but you have to invite Him in.

Day 283

Giving Advice

The true secret of giving advice is,
after you have honestly given it,
to be perfectly indifferent whether
it is taken or not and never persist
in trying to set people right.

HANNAH WHITALL SMITH

Day 284

Learning Names

Learn the names of everyone
around you and see each of them
as the most important person
at that very moment.

Day 285

Give Love

Hurting people hurt others,
which means they usually need as
much love as we can possibly give.

Day 286

Live within Your Means

No one admires a person
or the nice things they have that
are about to be repossessed.

Day 287
I Will Be with You

*"'I will be with you as I was
with Moses. I will not fail
you or abandon you.'"*

JOSHUA 1:5 NLT

Day 288

A Good Break

*Unrelenting disappointment leaves
you heartsick, but a sudden good
break can turn life around.*

PROVERBS 13:12 MSG

Day 289
Real Riches

Ordinary riches can be stolen,
real riches cannot. In your soul are
infinitely precious things that
cannot be taken from you.

OSCAR WILDE

Day 290

Be What You Are

Be what you are. This is
the first step toward becoming
better than you are.

JULIUS CHARLES HARE

Day 291

He Is the One

When it feels like the whole world walks out on you, know that He never left. You may not have recognized Him in the chaos and drama, but He is the One who matters most anyway.

Day 292

Help Others in Need

It's important to help others in need.
A generous gift is giving more than
is expected—more than is required.
The next time you have an opportunity
to give, open your heart wide and
give abundantly. You might be
surprised at the unexpected
return on your investment.

Day 293
Be Content

Contentment is merely being
fulfilled in what you have and who you
are. It's important to be content, while
pursuing all that God destined you
to become. Make contentment
a part of your journey.

Day 294

Wisdom

*Wisdom puts more strength
in one wise person than ten
strong men give to a city.*

ECCLESIASTES 7:19 MSG

Day 295

Laughter Is the Sun

Laughter is the sun that drives
winter from the human face.

VICTOR HUGO

Day 296

Make Every Minute Count

If you knew exactly how many
days you had left to live, would you
do anything differently? We can become
so busy with the little things that
we miss the big opportunities.
Make every minute count.

Day 297

Build Bridges

Build bridges in your life. Build bridges of reconciliation in your relationships. Bridge gaps between generations—between the young and old. You can become a voice for those who believe and those who do not.

Day 298
Who You Are

It is better to be hated for
what you are than to be loved for
something you are not.

ANDRE GIDE

Day 299

Wealth of Wisdom

*How much better it is to
get wisdom than gold! And to get
understanding is to be chosen above
silver. The highway of the upright is to
depart from evil; he who watches
his way preserves his life.*

Proverbs 16:16–17 NASB

Day 300

First Impressions

First impressions can deceive us.
Take care to guard your heart
and enter relationships with
your eyes open wide.

Day 301

Taking a Loss

The substance of the eminent
Socialist gentleman's speech is that
making a profit is a sin, but it is
my belief that the real sin
is taking a loss.

SIR WINSTON CHURCHILL

Day 302

Wise and Foolish

Wise men speak because they have something to say; fools because they have to say something.

PLATO

Day 303

True Experience

Someone can tell you about ice cream, but you can't understand it until you've had that cold and creamy experience on your tongue! It doesn't matter how much knowledge you have; there is nothing that can compare to the true experience.

Day 304

His Reflection

When people look, do you want
them to recognize your heavenly
Father's likeness? You can live
to mirror His reflection to others.
You can only do that if love
is the foundation of your life.

Day 305

God's Family

*Those who have been born into
God's family do not make a practice
of sinning, because God's life is in them.
So they can't keep on sinning, because
they are children of God.*

1 John 3:9 NLT

Day 306
The Gift of Grace

Grace doesn't expect repayment—
it is a gift given with no strings
attached. A wise man gives grace
knowing someday he might
need a little grace himself.

Day 307

Tell the Truth

You'll never get mixed up if
you simply tell the truth. Then you
don't have to remember what you
have said, and you never forget
what you have said.

SAM RAYBURN

Day 308

The Power of Prayer

Prayer provides direction,
guidance, and provision you need
to make the right choices for every
decision you face. Through the power
of prayer you can begin to understand
the character and nature of God,
and realize the difference His Word
can make in your life today.

Day 309

The Occasional Surprise

Allow space in your daily schedule
for the occasional surprise.

Day 310

God's Goodness

Your goodness springs from
God's goodness. Keep your heart
and mind aligned with Him.

Day 311

Serve the Lord

"Choose for yourselves this day whom you will serve, whether the gods which your fathers served that were on the other side of the River, or the gods of the Amorites, in whose land you dwell. But as for me and my house, we will serve the Lord."

JOSHUA 24:15 NKJV

Day 312

Confusion

Be careful not to confuse
your career with your life.

Day 313

The Calm Level of the Sea

I have seen the sea lashed
into fury and tossed into spray,
and its grandeur moves the soul of the
dullest man; but I remember that it is
not the billows, but the calm level
of the sea from which all heights
and depths are measured.

JAMES GARFIELD

Day 314

Assumptions

Assumptions can be dangerous.
Just ask the person who assumed the
tube next to the sink was toothpaste
when it was in fact pain relief cream.

Day 315

Love Your Siblings

It's important to love your
siblings without the "even if."

Day 316

Quitters and Winners

If you surround yourself with
quitters, you will eventually quit.
The same is true if you surround
yourself with winners,
you will eventually win.

Day 317

Train Yourself to Be Godly

Have nothing to do with godless myths and old wives' tales; rather, train yourself to be godly. For physical training is of some value, but godliness has value for all things, holding promise for both the present life and the life to come.

1 Timothy 4:7–8 NIV

Day 318

Never Give Up

Determination is a lot like superglue.
When you have the will to stick to
something, you will eventually
succeed. Pursue your dreams with
determination. Never give up.

Day 319

Love Liberty

I would rather belong to a poor nation that was free than to a rich nation that had ceased to be in love with liberty. But we shall not be poor if we love liberty, because the nation that loves liberty truly sets every man free to do his best.

WOODROW WILSON

Day 320

Love Looks Beyond

Love sees the whole person, not just the mistakes they've made. Love looks beyond who they are today to who they have the potential to become.

Day 321

A Tub of Bubbles

One way to beat stress is to settle deeply in a nice, hot, overflowing tub of bubbles.

Day 322

The Final Result

When inspiration and persistence
stand firm in the face of rejection, the
final result can only be achievement.

Day 323

Rain out of Heaven

Children of Zion, celebrate!
Be glad in your God. He's giving
you a teacher to train you how to live
right—Teaching, like rain out of heaven,
showers of words to refresh and nourish
your soul, just as he used to do.

JOEL 2:23 MSG

Day 324

A Positive Attitude

Complaints fuel a negative
atmosphere and affect everyone
in it. Disappointing circumstances
can become positive when you
maintain a positive attitude
and speak encouraging words.

Day 325

Repentance

Some people do not like to hear much of repentance; but I think it is so necessary that if I should die in the pulpit, I would desire to die preaching repentance, and if out of the pulpit, I would desire to die practicing it.

MATTHEW HENRY

Day 326

Pity the Fool

Never pity the fool who pities himself.

Day 327

Laughter

A daily dose of laughter will bring
light and life to your face and health
to your body and spirit.

Day 328

What You Think About

You become what you think about. Don't allow your mind to stay full of worries, cares, and negative thinking. Instead, recall the many blessings you have received

Day 329

In Vain

Unless the Lord builds the house,
they labor in vain who build it;
unless the Lord guards the city,
the watchman keeps awake in vain.

PSALM 127:1 NASB

Day 330

Things

There is nothing wrong with
people having things. The problem
comes when things have people.

Day 331

Eternal Blessings

A man may lose the good things of this life against his will; but if he loses the eternal blessings, he does so with his own consent.

AUGUSTINE

Day 332

The Gift of Encouragement

One of the greatest gifts you
can receive is encouragement.

Day 333

God's Creation

Take time to enjoy God's creation.
Don't miss a finger-painted sunset
that God created just for you.

Day 334

Stand Strong

Know what you believe, and when you are tempted you will be able to stand strong.

Day 335

Training and Instruction

Fathers, do not exasperate your children; instead, bring them up in the training and instruction of the Lord.

EPHESIANS 6:4 NIV

Day 336

Good Etiquette

Demonstrate good etiquette. Manners
show respect, care, and consideration.

Day 337

A Great Deal of Truth

We shall all see and understand a great deal of truth to which we are now blind, and then we shall be very thankful indeed that the Lord did not wait, nor refuse to accept us, until we could and would understand all that He meant us to know about Him.

HANNAH HURNARD

Day 338

Expect to Succeed

When we fail to expect,
we can keep faith from performing.

Day 339

A True Present

A true present is something
you work hard for in order to
give it to someone you love.

Day 340

Your Talents

Your abilities or talents are referred
to as gifts throughout the Bible.
He has given you gifts so that you
can give them to others.

Day 341

God's Plans

"Don't you see, you planned
evil against me but God used those
same plans for my good, as you
see all around you right now—
life for many people."

GENESIS 50:20 MSG

Day 342

People Are Remarkable

People have the ability to
look deep within themselves and
find whatever is necessary to rise to
the occasion and overcome the most
difficult of circumstances. Most likely
you have substance within you that
you don't even know about yet.

Day 343

Impatient People

Impatient people water their
miseries and hoe up their comforts;
sorrows are visitors that come
without invitation, and complaining
minds send a wagon to bring
their troubles home in.

CHARLES SPURGEON

Day 344

Appearance

It really doesn't matter what
people look like on the outside.

Day 345

Share Your Story

Stories of one another's triumphs can bring comfort and insight. Be willing to share your story with transparency.

Day 346

Be Generous

A tightfisted man gives what
he would otherwise throw away.
A generous man offers his
best even if he has to sacrifice.

Day 347

Your Portion of Power

The Lord is your portion of power.
The weaker you feel, the more
you can rely on Him. When you
are your weakest, allow Him
to be your strength.

Day 348

Eternal Gold

*All good athletes train hard.
They do it for a gold medal that
tarnishes and fades. You're after
one that's gold eternally.*

1 Corinthians 9:25 msg

Day 349

A Noble Heart

You may speak but a word
to a child, and in that child there
may be slumbering a noble heart
which shall stir the Christian
Church in years to come.

CHARLES SPURGEON

Day 350

Precious Prayer Time

Why spend that precious time
telling God all your worries—
things He already knows. Instead
give Him minutes of silence, moments
of praise and allow His wisdom to
penetrate your heart and direct
everything that concerns you.

Day 351

A Song of Praise

Let your life sing a song of
praise and adoration to God.

Day 352

Lessons in Life

All the lessons you could ever
learn mean little unless you know
the Greatest Teacher and Creator of
your very life. Only He could teach
you the most meaningful things
you really need to know.

Day 353

Your Presence

*You hide them in the
shelter of your presence.*

PSALM 31:20 NLT

Day 354

A Great Sense of Humor

When someone has to tell you they have a great sense of humor, they really mean they have no humor at all.

Day 355

Childlike

It is good to be children sometimes,
and never better than at Christmas,
when its mighty Founder
was a child Himself.

CHARLES DICKENS

Day 356

Experience the New

Sometimes we have to let go of the
old so we can experience the new.

Day 357

Taste Success

When you are determined
to learn something new,
the effort and patience become
indescribably satisfying as
you begin to taste success.

Day 358

Words Are Important

Consider the things you say before
you say them. Words are important
because someone is always listening.

Day 359

Trust in the Lord

Pride goes before destruction, a haughty spirit before a fall. Better to be lowly in spirit along with the oppressed than to share plunder with the proud. Whoever gives heed to instruction prospers, and blessed is the one who trusts in the LORD.

PROVERBS 16:18–20 NIV

Day 360

Successful

Those who are successful look for
the good in others, are thoughtful and
courteous of others, accept life in spite
of their circumstances, continue to
explore possibilities with hope.

Day 361

After Death

Everything science has taught me—
and continues to teach me—strengthens
my belief in the continuity of our
spiritual existence after death. Nothing
disappears without a trace.

WERNHER VON BRAUN

Day 362

Every Day Is Christmas

Live your life as if it were
Christmas every day.

Day 363

A Relationship with God

Just as God rejoices when we are reunited with Him in relationship through the gift of eternal life, we, too, have the hope of seeing those we love again, and even more in knowing we will one day touch the face of God.

Day 364

Your Audience

God is your audience of One!

Day 365

God's Mercy

But God—so rich is He in His mercy!
Because of and in order to satisfy
the great and wonderful and intense
love with which He loved us.

EPHESIANS 2:4 AMP

Notes:

Notes:
....
....
....
....
....
....
....
....
....
....
....

Notes:

Notes:

Notes:

Notes:

....

....

....

....

....

....

....

....

....

....

....

Notes:..
....
....
....
....
....
....
....
....
....
....
....